• GREEN GUIDE •

MARINE MAMMALS OF AUSTRALIA

Nigel Marsh

DEDICATION

In memory of my wonderful wife Helen Rose, you will live in my heart forever.

ACKNOWLEDGEMENTS

I would like to thank Paul Cross and the wonderful staff of Naturaliste Charters for introducing me to the amazing Killer Whales of the Bremer Canyon. Also, Scott Portelli and his Swimming with Gentle Giants operation in Tonga, where I had an incredible time snorkelling with Humpback Whales; the team from Dive Timor Lorosae for brilliant encounters with Pygmy Blue Whales and the other cetaceans of the Wetar Strait; and Albany's Historic Whaling Station at Discovery Bay.

I would also like to thank the amazing photographers who have shared their fabulous photos to make this guide a more complete book – thank you Cassandra Smith, Sandra Broom, John Natoli, Stanley Chan, Lisa Mazzella, Toby Dickson, Sergio Martinez, Justin Hofman and the numerous photographers from Shutterstock.

Images used in this book were taken under permit and with respect to the local Aboriginal and traditional peoples of the areas.

Published in 2026 by Reed New Holland Publishers
newhollandpublishers.com

A record of this book is held at the National Library of Australia.

ISBN 9781760796303

Managing Director: Fiona Schultz
Office manager: Olga Dementiev
Publisher and Project Editor: Simon Papps
Designer: Andrew Davies
Production Director: Arlene Gippert

Keep up with Reed New Holland
and New Holland Publishers
NewHollandPublishers
@newhollandpublishers and @ReedNewHolland

CONTENTS

Australian Sea Lion.

Killer Whales.

Dugong.

Spinner Dolphins.

INTRODUCTION TO AUSTRALIAN MARINE MAMMALS

Introduction

Australia is very fortunate to be home to an amazing variety of marine mammals. Whales and dolphins can be seen right around the nation, while in southern waters seals are common and in the north Dugongs frolic. Marine mammals are an important part of a healthy marine environment and spectacular to see in their natural habitat.

The abundant marine mammals of Australia traditionally provided a food source for the coastal Indigenous peoples. They had little impact on these animals, unlike the Europeans who arrived and almost hunted many to the brink of extinction.

Fortunately, all marine mammals are now fully protected around Australia, and in most cases their numbers are increasing. Today people take great joy from seeing these animals in the wild when whale watching, or when snorkelling or diving with these majestic creatures.

In this guide you will plunge deep into the world of Australia's marine mammals. Designed for anyone fascinated by whales, dolphins, seals and sea cows, this book is a great introduction to marine mammals, looking at species, biology, behaviour, threats and all aspects of the lives of these fascinating animals.

Indo-Pacific Bottlenose Dolphins are common in Australian waters.

How did marine mammals evolve?

Sperm Whale skeleton.

The skeleton of a Blue Whale.

There must have been something in the water around 50 million years ago, as it was at this time that three groups of marine mammals first entered the water. What drew them to the water is unknown, but it probably had something to do with food and getting away from land predators.

The evolution process took many millions of years, and saw numerous species come and go. Fossil records of these evolving animals have been found, showing changes to their bodies and limbs as they better adapted to life in the water. In the process they retained their mammalian traits; they breathed air, gave birth to live young and suckled their young, while their bodies changed dramatically to turn them into aquatic animals.

The seals changed the least, as they still live on land for much of their life. Seals retained their fur coats, with their main changes being their elongated and streamlined bodies and their limbs evolving into flippers. It is thought that seals evolved from bear-like animals, and are today most closely related to weasels, raccoons and skunks.

The cetaceans (whales, dolphins and porpoises) and sea cows (dugongs and manatees) underwent a much more complex evolution. They lost their coat of fur and instead developed thick body fat or blubber to stay warm. Their bodies became elongated and streamlined to make them more efficient in the water, their front limbs evolved into flippers, their rear limbs disappeared, and their tails flatten and widened. While the sea cows retained a head and neck, in the cetaceans the head fused with the body, the nostrils moved to the top of the head and their mouths greatly enlarged.

Cetaceans evolved from four-legged hoofed animals, and their closest living land relatives today are the hippos. It is thought that sea cows evolved from pig-like animals, and today their closest relatives on land are the elephants.

Different types of whales and dolphins

Whales, dolphins and porpoises are the only members of the infraorder Cetacea and are commonly called cetaceans as a group. This is a diverse group of aquatic animals that inhabits salt and fresh water, and seas from the tropics to polar regions. The group contains 94 species and is split into two subgroups based not on their size, but their dental arrangement.

The largest group is the toothed whales (parvorder Odontocetes). As the name suggests all these cetaceans have teeth so they can feed on fish, crustaceans, molluscs and, in the case of Killer Whales, other marine mammals. All the dolphins and porpoises are contained within this group, and so are many whales, such as the Sperm Whale, beaked whales, pilot whales and Killer Whale. Members of this group are unique in that they can use a form of sonar, known as echolocation, to bounce sound waves off objects to find them.

A False Killer Whale showing its teeth, which are a typical feature of the toothed whales.

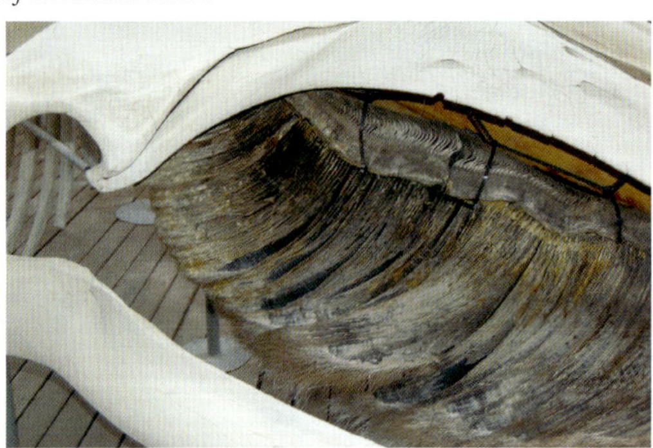

The hair-like baleen of a Humpback Whale.

The other group is the baleen whales (parvorder Mysticetes). These whales lack teeth and instead have a mouth lined with dense bristles, called baleen, that are made of keratin (the same substance in fingernails and hair). These whales use their baleen to filter food, swallowing large quantities of water to capture plankton, tiny crustaceans and small fishes. Most members of this group are huge, like the Blue Whale and Humpback Whale, and need to eat massive quantities of food. It is thought that the two groups split around 34 million years ago.

Different types of seals

The seals are another complex group of animals that is mostly found in cooler temperate waters, but a few inhabit tropical waters, and one is even found in fresh water. As a group they are known as pinnipeds, within the clade Pinnipedia, with 34 known species. The seals are split into three separate families based on shared characteristics.

The seal family Odobenidae contains only one species, the Walrus. Well-known for their large tusk teeth, this Northern Hemisphere species is not found in Australia.

The family Phocidae contains the earless or true seals, which have no visible ears. These seals having small flippers and move on land by crawling. Most Southern Hemisphere members of this family live in Antarctica or around the Subantarctic islands, although Southern Elephant Seals and Leopard Seals do turn up in southern Australia.

The most common seals in Australian waters are members of the family Otariidae, also known as the eared seals. The fur seals and sea lions are contained within this family, and all have visible ears and waddle on land with the aid of their flippers.

A colony of Australian Fur Seals at Montague Island.

Different types of sea cows

The sea cows are well named as they are grazing animals that eat vast quantities of seagrass. They belong to the order Sirenia, and are found in tropical and subtropical bays, rivers and estuaries where seagrasses grow. The group comprise two families and four surviving species.

The manatees, family Trichechidae, are only found in the Atlantic Ocean. The three members in this family are typically found in rivers, such as the Amazon River, or shallow coastal waters, and have a large, rounded, paddle-like tail.

The only surviving member of the family Dugongidae is the Dugong. This wide-ranging animal is found throughout the Indo-West Pacific but is most abundant in northern Australia. There are several characteristics that distinguish the Dugong from the manatees, with the main one being the tail shape, with the Dugong having a curved crescent-shaped tail like a dolphin. The only other member of this family was the Steller's Sea Cow, which grew to 10m long. Unfortunately, this species was hunted to extinction, disappearing in 1768.

The Dugong is a grazing marine mammal that eats seagrass.

A limited number of Dugongs are hunted by Indigenous people in Australia.

Marine mammals and indigenous people

The Indigenous peoples of Australia, the Aboriginal people and Torres Strait Islanders, traditionally consumed a wide range of foods, including marine mammals. The hunting of these animals was an important part of their custom and culture, and even depicted in their art.

Armed with spears and other weapons, the Indigenous peoples of the north regularly hunted Dugongs, while those living in the south preyed on seals. Dugong and seal bones have been found in coastal middens, where Indigenous people disposed of their refuse.

Whales and dolphins were much more difficult to hunt, and it is thought that they were mainly consumed after being washed ashore or stranded. A dead whale provided a feast for Indigenous people, and they tried to use every part of the carcass, with the ribs used to build huts and the ear bones used as drinking containers.

Today, traditional hunting practices by Indigenous peoples are still allowed across Australia. However, the Dugong is the only marine mammal that is regularly hunted. While these animals are listed as Endangered, Australia is home to the world's largest population of Dugongs, and it is thought that the small number hunted by Indigenous people each year is far less than are killed by gill nets, shark nets, boat strikes and habitat loss.

The bad old days of whaling and sealing

The large-scale hunting of whales and seals in Australia began as soon as Europeans settled in 1788. With an abundance of these marine mammals found around the southern coastline, whaling and sealing became a major industry and an important export for the growing colonies.

Whaling in those early days was a very dangerous and difficult business, as rowing boats and hand-thrown harpoons were used. Most whaling was done from shore or close to the coast from sailing boats, and they mostly hunted slow-moving whales, resting whales or mothers with calves. Sperm, Humpback and Southern Right Whales were the favoured targets, taken for their meat and oil.

The oil was the main prize, and it was derived from cooking whale blubber. It was used for burning in lanterns and lubricating machinery, and to make soap, paint and varnish. Later it was also used to produce margarine and cosmetics, and in car gearboxes. The most highly prized oil came from the heads of Sperm Whales.

Seals were mostly killed for their skins and were either shot or clubbed. The skins are waterproof and were prized for the making of jackets and boots. Sealers wiped out the Southern Elephant Seal populations of Tasmania and killed countless fur seals and sea lions. Unfortunately, Europeans killed so many seals that by 1802 there were so few left in the southern waters of Australia that they turned their attention to New Zealand.

An explosive harpoon gun, used to kill whales, on an old whaling vessel in a museum in Albany.

Whaling was much more profitable and became easier when steam-powered ships and harpoon guns came into use at the end of the 19th century. This allowed whaling ships to venture further from the coast, even to Antarctica, and to kill larger and faster-moving targets such as Blue, Fin and Sei Whales. Factory ships also went into service, so that the whales didn't have to be dragged back to port to be cut up and processed, allowing that grisly operation to happen at sea.

Older-style hand-thrown whaling harpoons in a museum on Norfolk Island.

As the larger whale populations declined, the whalers would target smaller species such as the minke whales. However, by the 1970s most whaling operations had shut around Australia. This was mainly because whaling had become unsustainable due to a lack of whales, and the oil harvested from whales could be sourced from other products. With protests from green groups and concerned citizens, whaling was finally outlawed in Australia in 1979.

The last Australian whaling station, the Cheynes Beach Whaling Company, closed in 1978. It is now preserved as a tourist attraction in Albany, Western Australia, as a reminder of the bad old days of whaling.

Whale meal (dried whale meat) bag in a museum on Norfolk Island.

Blue Whales are making a slow and steady recovery from whaling.

The slow recovery from whaling and sealing

By the time whaling and sealing stopped, the populations of these marine mammals in Australian waters had dramatically declined. It has been estimated that some whale species decreased from hundreds of thousands to only a few hundred, and it wasn't much better for the seals. While some whale and seal populations have recovered, others have sadly not.

The four species of seals that lived in southern Australia have had very different stories after sealing stopped. Although most large-scale sealing stopped by 1825, seals were still killed, especially by fishers in nets and because they were considered competition for fish. Several acts to protect seals were put in place by state governments, but the animals weren't fully protected across Australia until 1999.

Both Australian Fur Seal and Longnose Fur Seal have experienced remarkable recoveries, with steady increases in population each year. Unfortunately, the Australian Sea Lion is the opposite. Its numbers may have slowly recovered after sealing stopped, but the population is sadly in declined again, dropping by 60 per cent during the last 40 years due to fishing pressures. The species is now listed as Endangered. Unfortunately, the fourth seal species that used to be found in southern Australia – the Southern Elephant Seal – has never re-established colonies back in the country.

The Australian Sea Lion is still threatened by current fishing practices.

Whale species have fortunately increased in numbers since whaling ceased. Some, such as the Blue Whale and Southern Right Whale, have had a slow and modest increase in numbers, while others, notably the Humpback Whale, have surprised everyone with the speed of their recovery, especially in recent years. The Australian population of Humpback Whales, seen off both the west and east coasts, is the largest in the world and increasing at a rate of 10 per cent per year. The migrating population is currently estimated to be around 60,000 off the west coast and 40,000 off the east coast, which is an incredible turnaround from a population of only a few hundred in the 1960s.

Threats to marine mammals

Since the end of whaling and sealing, most marine mammal populations have regrown to healthy levels. However, many other threats have emerged that can cause harm and death to these majestic ocean animals.

One of the biggest threats is fishing nets. A variety of nets are used by the fishing industry, and while people try to make them as safe as possible, they still entangle and drown marine mammals. The Australian Sea Lion population continues to fall as too many animals are killed in nets each year. Nets also kill dolphins and dugongs. Overfishing has also depleted numbers of the fish and squid that many marine mammals feed on, and in Antarctica the large-scale fishing of krill is threatening the food supply of many baleen whales.

In Australia, shark nets at swimming beaches are designed to kill sharks, however, they also kill dugongs, dolphins and whales. Each winter Humpback Whales get entangled in shark nets. While most get free with the aid of humans, it would be best if the nets were removed over the winter months when the whales are migrating.

Pollution, collisions and climate change

Pollution also impacts on marine mammals. Pollutants in the water and food chain, from agricultural and industrial runoff, can lead to sickness and death. Additionally, plastics in the water are one of the biggest killers of marine mammals. It is estimated that more than 100,000 marine mammals die each year due to plastics, either from eating them or from becoming entangled in them.

A global increase in large cargo ships has also resulted in an increase in collisions with marine mammals. Whales at the surface have been killed or injured by large ships. However, even small boats can cause injuries to seals, dolphins and dugongs through lacerations caused by propeller blades. Oil spills from ships also kill marine mammals. And an increase in ships has led to more noise pollution in the ocean, confusing their echolocation and making it harder for dolphins and whales to communicate with each other and navigate.

This unfortunate Dugong was killed by a boat strike.

Climate change is also affecting marine mammals. A rise in sea temperatures will impact on the food they eat and their migration patterns, as well as having a range of implications for marine habitats.

Captive marine mammals

The keeping of marine mammals is a controversial topic that is declining in support each year. While some argue that they are breeding these marine mammals to protect them, the simple truth is that most are kept in artificial environments for entertainment and to make money.

A wide variety of whales, dolphins and seals are kept in captivity and have been for more than 100 years. While conditions have improved in most of these facilities in countries such as Australia, many animals still die in other countries when captured, transported or housed in substandard aquariums.

Common Bottlenose Dolphins in an oceanarium in Japan.

Whales and dolphins are wide-ranging species that can travel hundreds of kilometres in a day. Unfortunately, even the largest of aquariums are tiny compared to their natural habitat. Some are kept in concrete pools that are easy to maintain and easier for the public to view the animals. While others are kept in ocean pens in bays, that are generally larger and more natural, but these can expose the animals to boat noises and a range of pollutants. While it may appear that seals adapt far better to being kept in captivity, a small pool and pen does not compare to the open ocean and living in the wild.

Marine mammals in captivity don't get as much activity and exercise as they would in the wild, so they can become overweight and have health issues. They also get bored, and while they are made to do tricks to entertain the public, these tricks do not replicate natural behaviour. Captive animals also tend to get sick and suffer from stress, and some have become unnaturally aggressive and attacked people.

Facilities in Australia that keep marine mammals do a great deal of conservation work. They help animals that get caught in nets or stranded, and rehabilitate sick and injured animals. They also don't capture new animals to exhibit, as most are captive-bred.

With it so easy to see wild dolphins, whales and seals around the coastline of Australia, is there any reason to have these animals kept in captivity for entertainment and profit?

Wild Australian Humpback Dolphin being fed at Tin Can Bay.

Should people feed wild dolphins?

In Australia it is illegal to feed dolphins in the wild. However, there are four sites around the nation that have a special permit enabling people to handfeed these marine mammals. While it is a great way for people to get close to wild cetaceans, the handfeeding of dolphins is a contentious issue.

Humans have been feeding dolphins for thousands of years, either directly or indirectly. Dolphins are smart animals, and many have worked out that they can get a free meal from fishers, from stealing from nets or following fishing boats. In the past many fishers enjoyed having dolphins around and threw them a fish or two, which led to them becoming friendly and revisiting the fishers regularly. This is how most dolphin-feeding activities begin.

In Australia, dolphins are handfed at Monkey Mia and Bunbury in Western Australia and at Tin Can Bay and Tangalooma in Queensland. There are strict rules at these feeding sites to protect the dolphins, with them only fed a small number of fish. This means that the dolphins must catch additional prey to feed themselves, and don't lose their hunting skills. Dolphin feeds in Australia attract thousands of tourists each year, so are great for the local economy, although researchers say that they are not so great for the dolphins.

Researchers have several concerns with the practice, with their studies showing that fed or provisioned dolphins have a smaller range than normal,

A warning sign at the Tin Can Bay dolphin feed.

as they stay close to the feeding site. This impacts on the development of young dolphins, as a smaller range means they don't get the social interaction with other dolphins that they need. Also, with a smaller range, there is a reduced area to capture prey, and more chance of an environment issue, such as a seagrass dieback, having more impact.

Studies have also found that some females that were fed from an early age become poor mothers, without the proper skills to feed and nurse their offspring. Researchers found that fed dolphins have lower reproductive success and a higher mortality rate for calves.

Many would like to see the handfeeding of dolphins phased out, but with this practice worth millions of dollars to the local economies of these sites, it is unlike to happen anytime soon.

Indo-Pacific Bottlenose Dolphins at Monkey Mia.

How do whales and dolphins use sonar?

The toothed whales, which includes the dolphins and porpoises, mostly eat fish and squid, and to find their prey in murky water or the dark waters of the deep ocean they use their own form of sonar, called echolocation.

All these cetaceans have a rounded forehead, called a melon, filled with fatty tissues, and via nasal sacs in their head they can send out rapid high-frequency clicks. The melon helps to focus these sound waves in front of the animal. With water being denser than air these sound waves travel rapidly and bounce off any object, returning to the animal as echoes.

The cetacean then receives these echoes in a fatty deposit located between the lower jaw and the ears, allowing the brain to interpret the result. From these echoes the animal can determine the object size, shape, speed and distance, and even its internal structure.

Echolocation is also used for navigation, allowing cetaceans to identify rocks and other obstacles. Cetaceans are not the only animals to use echolocation as bats also use these sound waves to hunt and navigate.

All toothed whales, such as these Indo-Pacific Bottlenose Dolphins, use sonar to find food and to navigate.

Why do seals have whiskers?

All seals have long thick whiskers on their snout, just like cats. While seals have good vision and hearing, which they use in and out of the water, one of their most important senses is touch, with their whiskers playing a vital role.

When seals hunt at night, in murky water or in deep dark water, they can't use their vision to find food and instead rely on their whiskers. These whiskers are very sensitive to vibrations, which allows seals to detect any movement by a fish. These whiskers are so sensitive that the seal can identify different fish species and the fish's size, and can even follow the wake of a fish that has passed up to

35 seconds before.

A seal's whiskers can even detect the gill movements of fish that are buried in the sand or hiding under rocks. When hunting, seals push their whiskers forward to give themselves the best chance of finding prey. Even blind seals can find food by using their whiskers.

Seals also use their whiskers on land when communicating to other seals. They extend them forward as a sign of aggression, and females often bite the whiskers of over-friendly males to drive them away.

Australian Fur Seals have sensitive whiskers that they use to find prey.

How do marine mammals stay warm?

Many whales, dolphins and seals swim and feed in polar regions, which have the coldest waters on Earth. With the water temperate around zero, and with water being a great heat conductor, sucking the body warmth out of any animal, these marine mammals have found the best way to stay warm is with a thick layer of fat, called blubber.

Whales, dolphins and seals, like all mammals, are warm blooded and have a body temperature between 35 and 38°C, depending on the species. To maintain that temperate in cold water they have an insulating layer of blubber under their skin. Fat is a poor conductor of heat, so the blubber stops these mammals losing body heat to the cold water.

In seals this blubber layer

Australian Fur Seals have both blubber and fur to keep them warm.

can be up to 10cm thick, while in dolphins it is around 5cm thick. The thickness of blubber varies among whales, with the larger baleen whales having the thickest blubber, up to 30cm thick. Marine mammals that live in warmer temperate and tropical waters don't need as much insulation, so have a much thinner layer of blubber.

In seals, blubber envelops the body, except for the head and flippers. To reduce heat loss, seals can limit blood flow in these areas. Seals also have fur to insulate them. While this fur does keep them a little warmer when in the water, it is more useful on land, with air trapped among the hairs keeping them warm when cold winds are blowing.

Why are baleen whales so big?

The baleen whales are some of the biggest animals to have ever lived, being longer and heavier than the dinosaurs. Scientists wondered for many years why these whales got so big.

At one time it was thought that some of the baleen whales evolved into huge animals due to competition for food and to keep them safe from large predators. However, it is now thought to have more to do with the last great ice age, with the large baleen whales developing around 4.5 million years ago.

Scientists have theorised that the whales grew bigger as the world got colder so they could eat large quantities of food quickly, and store that as fat in their huge bodies for months as they travelled long distances between feeding and breeding grounds. By getting larger they fared much better than many smaller baleen whales, with some going extinct during this period.

However, with the effects of climate change, there is now a worry that these large whales will not do well if the oceans warm, with less food for them to feast on in polar regions.

The Blue Whale is the largest animal to have ever lived – even bigger than the largest dinosaur.

Deep-diving marine mammals

Marine mammals breathe air and come to the surface to take regular breaths. While all marine mammals can hold their breath for much longer than a human, some can remain underwater for more than an hour as they dive very deep to find food.

Dugongs are the least adapted to deep diving as they feed on seagrasses in shallow bays. They generally go no deeper than 30m and can hold their breath for around six minutes.

Seals are better adapted to diving deep. While Australian Sea Lions mostly hunt in shallow water, Australian Fur Seals dive to depths of 200m for up to seven minutes, and Longnose Fur Seals dive to 380m for up to 15 minutes. The best deep diver among the seals is the Southern Elephant Seal, which can dive to 2,388m for up to two hours.

The Short-finned Pilot Whale can dive to depths of 1,000m to feed on squid and fish.

Whale diving strategies

Baleen whales mostly feed at the surface, so generally don't dive too deep or for too long. On the other hand, many toothed whales dive very deep to find prey. While most dolphins feed in shallow or surface waters, the Striped Dolphin can dive to 700m. Short-finned Pilot Whales can dive to 1,000m for up to 20 minutes, while Sperm Whales can dive to 2,250m for more than an hour. However, the champion deep divers are the beaked whales, with the Cuvier's Beaked Whale able to dive to 3,000m for more than three hours!

As marine mammals evolved, one of the changes that took place was in their myoglobin, which binds oxygen and iron proteins found in cardiac and muscle tissue. Researchers discovered that marine mammals carry much more oxygen in their myoglobin than land mammals, enabling them to hold their breath for longer and dive deeper. As they dive, they can also slow their heart rate to conserve oxygen.

Diving deep exerts enormous pressures on the bodies of marine mammals. To avoid damage to their organs they have flexible ribcages, and their lungs can compress. Blubber also helps to absorb pressure on their organs. However, marine mammals can develop decompression sickness, or the bends, the same as scuba divers, from nitrogen bubbles expanding as they ascend too quickly. To avoid the bends, they ascend slowly from deep dives.

Why do whales and dolphins strand?

The news of a single whale or dolphin washed up on a beach is always sad, but even more so when it happens to large groups of cetaceans. The reasons for the stranding of whales and dolphins are not fully understood, but there may be several factors involved.

When whales and dolphins are sick or injured, they often head into shallow water to convalesce. Unfortunately, in this vulnerable state they can get washed up on a beach if the weather turns foul, the tides change or if they get confused. This generally explains how single animals get stranded.

As whales and dolphins are social animals and often travel in a group, when one animal gets in trouble the others in the group try to help it. This can result in a group of animals ending up being stranded when they go to aid a sick member of the group.

However, many mass stranding occur in the same area. In these cases, it is possible that the topography, such as a sloping sandy seafloor, can cause the stranding by confusing the animal's echolocation. And once one animal is trapped, the others follow to help it.

Other possible causes of mass stranding include navy ships using sonar, underwater seismic activity, magnetic-field anomalies and even diseases or parasites in the ears or sinuses.

Hundreds of human volunteers generally arrive at the scene of a mass stranding to help the whales and dolphins back into the water. Sometimes these actions succeed, but sadly sometimes they don't.

A dead Eden's Whale on a beach. The reason for the stranding was unclear.

A male Humpback Whale in singing position with its head down.

The songs of humpback whales

All whales and dolphins make noises that can be heard underwater. Most of these noises are clicks, whistles, grunts, snorts, moans and groans. However, there is one whale that is blessed with an ability to combine these sounds into a complex and haunting melodic song – the Humpback Whale.

Only the male Humpbacks sing, mostly during the breeding season, and their songs generally last from a few minutes to half an hour, but sometimes for several hours. When the male sings he hovers in midwater with his head down. Mostly the singer is alone, but occasionally he is joined by other silent males. All the males in the area sing the same song, with only a few slight differences. However, the songs change gradually from season to season. The songs can be heard up to 10km away, so are overheard by every whale in the area.

When whales evolved from land mammals their larynx modified so they could make sounds underwater. Baleen whales, like the humpback, don't have vocal cords, instead they have a U-shaped tissue in the voice box with a large cushion of fat and muscle. This cushion vibrates when the whale exhales air and generates sound.

Why Humpback Whales sing their haunting songs is not known. Singers don't appear to attract females, as once thought, yet do attract other males. The songs are not used to establish dominance, but sometimes another male will disrupt a singer. It could be simply used to communicate with other whales and to attract females to an area. It has also been noted that there is less singing now that the Humpback Whale population has grown since whaling ended, so the songs might be less important now for whale communication.

Unfortunately, these wonderful songs are often drowned out by the louder sounds made by large ships, with an impact on the whales that is unknown.

Whale migrations

Whales undergo some of the longest migrations on Earth, with some travelling from polar regions to the tropics and back each year. Some whales travel more than 20,000km during these annual migrations.

While some toothed whales migrate with changes in the seasons, most of their movements are generally shorter than their cousins, the baleen whales. Most baleen whales spend the summer months feasting in rich polar waters. Then, having fattened up for many months, they head to breeding and birthing grounds in the tropics during the winter months.

Humpback Whales passing the Sunshine Coast on their annual migration.

The Humpback Highway

The best-known migration is that of the Humpback Whale. The ones seen off Australia migrate from Antarctica and head up the east and west coasts, known as the Humpback Highway, over the winter months. During these migrations to warmer waters the whales don't usually feed, instead living off their fat reserves. Mother Humpbacks that are feeding calves can lose up to half of their body weight during the migration.

It is thought that the females head to warmer waters to give birth and give their calves the best chance of survival. Raising a playful calf is probably easier in warm water as it builds its strength, skills and confidence, plus it is also safer as fewer Killer Whales are found in the tropics. However, the main reason for raising the calf in warmer waters is to give it time to grow and build up a layer of blubber before returning to the cold polar waters.

Adult male Humpback Whales have one reason to migrate, breeding. They follow the females to their warmer birthing waters as this is where the females are receptive to breeding.

However, not all Humpback Whales migrate each year, as some females in non-breeding years remain in the polar regions and fatten up for the next breeding migration.

Antarctic visitors

Whales are not the only visitors Australia receives from Antarctica, as each year several wayward seals visit our shores.

Leopard Seals travel great distances looking for food. They normally feed around the pack ice of Antarctica, but also hunt around the Subantarctic islands as well. However, each year several of these seals turn up along the coastline of Australia.

Leopard Seals mostly visit Australia in winter and spring, and most of these seals are subadults that have become lost. They haul onto beaches for a few days of rest and then head back to the cold waters of Antarctica.

Prior to Europeans arriving in Australia, Southern Elephant Seals could be found on several islands around Tasmania. Unfortunately, sealers wiped them out and now they only visit Australia from their breeding colonies on Subantarctic islands.

Elephant arrivals

Each year dozens of huge Southern Elephant Seals arrive on the beaches of southern Australia for a few days of relaxing and recreation. They mostly arrive at the end of summer, when moulting, and stay out of the water for a week or so while they shed their old fur coat. While most are happy to stay on a beach and sleep during this time, others like to see the sights and make a nuisance of themselves.

A well-watched Southern Elephant Seal at Portland, Victoria, named by admirers as 'Sammy'.

These curious Southern Elephant Seals venture beyond the beach and end up on roads, boat ramps and even in suburban yards. Some have been known to damage cars and other property. Most move on after a few weeks, but there is one Southern Elephant Seal – affectionately known as 'Neil' – that has been hanging around Tasmania since 2020.

Neil was born in Salem Bay, Tasmania, in October 2020, and since then has called Tasmania home and has become an internet star. He turns up at different spots around the state – moulting in Hobart, knocking down a fence in Dunalley or sunbaking at Kingston Beach. He has been moved on numerous times for his own safety after drawing too much attention from people and dogs.

Are dolphins and porpoises the same?

Dolphins and porpoises are both cetaceans and members of the toothed whale group. They might look similar, but are different in several ways, so placed in separate families.

There are eight known species of porpoise, and they range in size from 1.3m to 2.3m. They differ from dolphins in having a rounded head with no beak and having spade-shaped teeth, unlike the dolphin's conical teeth. They are also much less social and rarely found in groups.

Porpoises feed on fish and squid, like dolphins, and are found in tropical to polar waters, and inhabit rivers, bays, estuaries and the open ocean. No porpoise species are found in Australian waters.

Why do dolphins bow ride boats?

Dolphins seem to spend a lot of time playing. They are often observed leaping from the water and doing twists and turns, riding waves and even playing pass-the-parcel with pieces of seaweed. One of the most common fun activities they do is riding the bow waves of boats.

Dolphins are always busy travelling to different feeding areas, with groups almost constantly on the move. Dolphins, being intelligent creatures, are always looking for ways to save energy, and a free ride on a boat's bow wave is not to be passed up when travelling to the next meal.

When a boat moves through water it creates a pressure differential in the water, or a pressure wave. Dolphins know all about pressure waves as they have been riding them for millions of years, using ones created by travelling whales. By positioning themselves in front of the boat they can ride these waves, like a body surfer, and save energy in what is known as hydroplaning.

Large ships create big pressure waves, allowing a large group of dolphins to ride the pressure wave. However, even small boats can get up to a dozen dolphins riding these waves. When hydroplaning, the dolphins often turn upside down and click and whistle to each other. While bow riding is mainly used to save energy, dolphins seem to have a lot of fun hydroplaning in front of boats.

A group of Indo-Pacific Bottlenose Dolphins enjoying a bow ride.

A spectacular breach from an adult Humpback Whale.

Why do whales breach?

Some whale species spend a great deal of time at the surface with parts of their body exposed in the air. They lift their heads from the water, which is known as spy-hopping, and also wave their fins and tail in the air and slap them on the surface. However, the most dramatic whale performance is a breach.

Breaching is when a whale leaps from the water and crashes back with a mighty explosion of whitewater. Some of these breaches expose only half the body, but the most spectacular involve a full body breach.

Humpback Whales are the best-known breachers, as they are often observed by whale-watching boats. However, many other whale species also breach. Humpbacks can do a single breach, several, or a dozen or more, but some have been recorded performing more than 100 in a row. Sometimes a single whale does the breaching, but often several can be involved, including mothers and calves.

There are several possible reasons why whales breach. They may do it to remove parasites, such as barnacles and remoras. Other theories postulate that it may also be done to stun prey, to spy on boats, to communicate with other whales, or as a way of showing off. Or it could simply be for fun, as young Humpbacks often breach around their mother. Whatever the reason, it is spectacular to watch a whale breaching.

Marine mammal reproduction

The sex lives of marine mammal are very complex and differ greatly between the different families and species. Some males and females live separately and only come together to reproduce. In other species individuals mate with multiple partners, and some dolphins even have sex just for pleasure.

Male and female Dugongs look identical, and with their genitals hidden away in a slit there is no easy way to tell them apart. They are mostly solitary animals that only come together to feed and breed. In the breeding season males establish a territory and sometimes fight to determine dominance. Females that are ready to mate visit these territories. A group of males will follow a receptive female and fight each other, and some even rough up the female, leaving scars with their tusk-like teeth. When mating, the male grips the female from underneath.

Differing seal strategies

Reproduction among seals varies greatly. Fur seal and elephant seal males establish a territory on a beach or rocky shoreline and fight rival males to maintain their patch. The smaller females then arrive and fight among themselves for their own patch within the male's territory. The females then give birth to last season's pup, and around a week later the female fur seals mate with the male, while female elephant seals mate about three weeks after giving birth. Female fur seals can delay implantation of the fertilised egg for up to three months, so they can time the birth to coincide with the next breeding season.

Like Dugongs, most whale and dolphin males and females look very similar, as they too have their genitals tucked away in a slit. This makes them more streamlined in the water.

Dolphins mostly breed over the summer months, and while the males don't establish territories, they do compete to mate by fighting. Groups of males will chase females, even herding them into shallow water, hoping to mate.

A large male Longnose Fur Seal with his harem of females.

A male Humpback Whale chasing a female in a breeding strategy called a heat run.

When a female is ready, she will display her genital slit to the chosen male. They then swim belly to belly as they mate. They will often mate several times and both mate with other partners.

Male baleen whales battle it out for the right to mate as they chase females. These huge whales ram, headbutt and tail slap each other in a contest, known as a heat run, to prove who is the best and strongest to win the female. Like dolphins, they mate belly to belly, and both the males and females mate with several partners during the breeding season.

Nursing young

Performing fatherly duties is not high on the agenda for male marine mammals, so it is up to the mother to feed and raise her young. Female marine mammals do an incredible job of looking after their young, having to feed them, teach them and protect them from predators.

All marine mammal mothers feed their young with milk. This milk is super rich in fats, which allows the young to grow quickly and build up a layer of blubber to keep them warm. Seal mothers feed their young on land and have nipples that the pups suckle. Dugongs have nipples that are located under their flippers. Dolphins and whales also have nipples that are hidden away in two mammary slits, located each side of their genital slit. When a calf is feeding the milk is ejected into the water and consumed.

How long the young are nursed by their mother varies greatly from species to species. Most seals only feed and nurse their pups for a few months, after which they go their separate ways and the young must look after themselves. In contrast, baby Dugongs suckle for more than a year and stay with their mother until they are sexually mature, which is generally at around eight years of age.

A young Australian Sea Lion suckling from its resting mother.

Dolphin young stick close to their mother, as with this pair of Fraser's Dolphins.

Dolphins and toothed whales also suckle their young for more than a year, and as many live in family groups they never really separate after they are weaned. Baleen whales suckle their young from six months to a year, and after that period most mothers and young part ways.

The bonds between mother and young are very strong in marine mammals. While seals separate from their young to go off and feed, young dolphins and dugongs always stick close to mum. Dolphin and whale females often work together to look after young calves, protecting them from predators. They will also look after another female's calf if the mother must dive deep to find food, and sometimes even suckling each other's offspring.

Marine mammal predators

While humans have recently been the top predator of marine mammals, there are a few animals that feed on them as well, including a few marine mammals that feed on each other.

Several shark species feed on marine mammals. In tropical waters Tiger Sharks are known to prey on dugongs and dolphins, and they also feast on dead whales. In cooler southern waters, Broadnose Sevengill Sharks are known to prey on seals. While a few whaler shark species, such as the Bull Shark, also prey on smaller marine mammals, the main shark species that feeds on marine mammals is the Great White Shark.

Great White Sharks hunt fur seals and sea lions around the southern coastline of Australia. The seals can easily outswim a Great White if it is spotted, so the sharks lurk below and take the seals by surprise in a lightning-fast attack. Great White Sharks also feed on dolphins and small whales, and are quickly on the scene when a dead whale surfaces.

The most common shark species to attack marine mammals is the very strange Cookie Cutter Shark. These sharks live in open water and only grow to 50cm long, and while they don't kill their prey, they like to take a plug of flesh from their victim. Many whales, dolphins and even seals are seen with circular scars made by the bite of the vicious little Cookie Cutter Shark.

Cetacean predators

False Killer Whales have been recorded feeding on dolphins and small whales, but their cousin the Killer Whale is the most notorious predator of marine mammals. While resident Killer Whales mostly feed on fish, transient popula-

The Great White Shark is one of the main predators to feed on marine mammals.

tions that roam open waters feed on just about anything, including seals, dolphins and other whales.

Hunting in packs they are very efficient predators, able to exhaust their prey by chasing it and disabling with bites to the fins, tail and stomach. They even tackle very large prey such as Blue Whales. Killer Whales are not the nicest of cetaceans, as they will sometimes kill other whales and only eat the tongue and lower jaw. They have also been known to play with their food, flicking injured seals into the air with their tail or throwing them with their mouth. Killer Whales have been known to kill seals and dolphins and not even eat them.

However, Killer Whales don't get it all their own way, as Sperm Whales and Humpback Whales have been observed to close ranks to protect calves from attack, and pilot whales have also been seen working together to chase off Killer Whales.

Whale watching

With whales seen around the coastline of Australia, especially during the winter months, whale watching is a popular activity and a big business worth more than 30 million dollars to the Australian economy each year. While you can watch whales from headlands and beaches, dedicated whale-watching tours get you much closer to the animals.

Whale watching in Australia started in Hervey Bay in Queensland in the 1980s, when a local fisherman noticed an increase in Humpback Whales gathering in the sheltered waters of the bay to rest on their journey back to Antarctica. He decided to take people out to see the whales and quickly established a very successful business.

Today Hervey Bay is recognised as the home of whale watching in Australia, with a fleet of dedicated whale-watching boats operating each winter and spring. The operators in Hervey Bay have set a global standard for environmental awareness and sustainable whale watching, and in 2019 it was declared the world's first Whale Heritage Area.

Key sites

Whale watching has steadily grown in popularity, with people now able to view Humpbacks off Hervey Bay, Sunshine Coast, Brisbane and Gold Coast in Queensland. In New South Wales, boats operate from Byron Bay, Coffs Harbour, Port Stephens, Sydney, Jervis Bay, Narooma and Eden. While in Western Australia, trips operate from Augusta, Dunsborough, Perth and Exmouth.

Humpbacks are the most popular whale to watch, as they spend a great deal of the time at the surface, and also fin- and tail-slap, breach and spy-hop. Some are so friendly and curious that they come right up to the boat. On these trips you also have a chance of seeing dolphins, Dwarf Minke Whales and, in more southerly waters, Southern Right Whales.

Southern Right Whales are more commonly seen along the southern coastline from boat and shore. These whales enter shallow bays and come in very close to shore with their calves. South Australia is the best place to view Southern Right

Whales, particularly off Victor Harbour and from the cliffs of the Great Australian Bight near Yalata. In Victoria they are viewed off Warrnambool and Portland, in Western Australia off Albany and in Tasmania off Bruny Island.

The big one

Mighty Blue Whales can also be viewed off Geographic Bay in Western Australia. Each November and December these whales are sighted on whale-watching trips from Dunsborough.

There is also a chance of seeing Blue Whales at one of the most exciting whale-watching locations in Australia – the Bremer Canyon. Located off Bremer Bay in Western Australia, the Bremer Canyon is a series of deep-water canyons that attract an incredible variety of marine life during summer and autumn. Whale-watching trips to this area also see Long-finned Pilot Whale, Sperm Whale and a variety of beaked whales and dolphins. However, the main attraction is Killer Whales, which hunt the other whales in the area and come very close to the boats at times.

Most of the whale-watching boats in Australia are also involved in research work, which is invaluable to ongoing studies of whales. They photograph the whales, especially distinguishing marks on their bodies and tail, and document how many whales they see, what the animals were doing, and how long the encounters last. Researchers are often on board these vessels to collect data and share information with the public.

A Killer Whale comes in close to a whale-watching boat in the Bremer Canyon.

Most underwater encounters with dolphins are very brief.

Snorkelling with whales and dolphins

Seeing a whale from the surface is a spectacular experience, however seeing one of these giants underwater is an event that you will never forget.

There are regulations in place around Australia to stop boats, drones, surfers, swimmers, snorkellers and divers getting too close to whales. These rules were put in place to avoid harassing resting whales, especially mothers with calves. However, several tourism operators have special permits that allow people to snorkel with whales, or they work within the guidelines of the regulations.

In Australia, people can snorkel with Humpback Whales during the winter months at Ningaloo Reef in Western Australia, off Hervey Bay and Mooloolaba in Queensland, and off Byron Bay, Coffs Harbour and Jervis Bay in New South Wales. Working within the regulations, these operators drop snorkellers in front of travelling whales. Then you wait on the surface and hope that the whales don't change course or dive deep before you see them. While a bit hit and miss, it is still an incredible experience to see a 15m-long whale swim past, even if it is for only a few brief seconds.

Occasionally longer encounters occur, when an inquisitive whale swims up to the snorkellers for a better look. While you are not allowed to swim towards or touch the whale, the whales can come to you and sometimes they have been known to circle a snorkeller for more than 10 minutes!

Which species?

While snorkelling with giant Humpback Whales is incredible, the best underwater whale encounters happen on the Ribbon Reefs, north of Cairns, in June and July, when the Dwarf Minke Whales come to play. These small baleen whales are the most curious and inquisitive of all the whales and seek out boats, divers and snorkellers.

Several dive operators have permits to place people in the water with these playful whales. And rather than having to look for the whales, the whales find the boats and hang around. The crew then run out ropes with floats, and snorkellers then quietly enter the water, spread along the ropes and wait for the Dwarf Minke Whales to come to them.

At times a dozen of more of these 6m-long whales can circle a boat and the snorkellers, and encounters can last for hours. At first the whales are a little shy, but slowly, with each pass, they get closer and closer. Often they come within a metre of the snorkellers for an unforgettable whale encounter.

Snorkelling with dolphins is also regulated in Australia. While dolphins can turn up just about anywhere, organised dolphins swim are available in Port Phillip Bay in Victoria, Port Stephens in New South Wales, Adelaide and Kangaroo Island in South Australia, and Bunbury and Rockingham in Western Australia.

Being in the water with dolphins is a great deal of fun. They are fast moving and often come in very close, and if you listen you will hear their range of clicks, grunts and whistles as they communicate and echolocate. All of these swims are with Indo-Pacific Bottlenose Dolphins, which is the most common species in Australia.

A snorkeller enjoys a close encounter with a Dwarf Minke Whale.

Snorkelling and diving with seals

Seals on land are rather clumsy animals that drag, waddle and crawl, while in the water they are graceful, fluid and highly manoeuvrable. They are also curious, playful and underwater acrobats, making them one of the most exciting animals to snorkel and dive with.

Like other marine mammals, there are rules and regulations about approaching seals in boats, on land and in the water. Breeding colonies are best avoided, as you are not allowed near the pups, and these are where Great White Sharks feed. Fortunately, there are many non-breeding haul-out sites and colonies where people can safely snorkel and dive with seals, without the risk of encountering a Great White Shark.

Seal snorkels with Australian Sea Lions are popular in Western Australia at Rockingham, Perth and Jurien Bay. You can also snorkel with this species in South Australia at Port Lincoln and Kangaroo Island. Snorkelling with Australian Fur Seals is possible in Port Phillip Bay in Victoria and at Montague Island off Narooma in New South Wales.

Snorkelling with both these species is a great deal of fun. The seals zoom around you and enjoy it when you do more than simply stare at them, so wave your arms and do somersaults and they will often copy you. They are a wild animal, so never try to pat them, and while they sometimes nibble on flippers, they rarely bite. The Australian Sea Lions are particularly playful and like to closely inspect you, and will rest on the bottom and gaze at you with their puppy-dog eyes.

Diving with seals is even more fun and there are even more places you can do this in southern Australia. Being on scuba is slightly more cumbersome, but allows you to be in deeper water with the seals and watch them playing with each other, chasing fish or even biting the tails of stingrays.

An Australian Fur Seal rests on the bottom to investigate a diver.

Dugong encounters

Dugongs are shy creatures that often live and feed in murky inshore bays and estuaries, so they can be difficult animals to observe in the wild. However, you can see them on boat tours in Shark Bay in Western Australia and in Moreton Bay off Brisbane.

On these trips tourists get to see Dugongs feeding and breathing at the surface. They are often initially spotted due to the cloud of silt they stir up when feeding on seagrass, and then you just have to wait several minutes for the animal to surface and take a breath. Dugongs don't expose much of themselves at the surface, so all you will see is the snout.

Underwater encounters with Dugongs are extremely rare. Divers have had brief encounters at dive sites off Queensland and Western Australia, which generally don't last for more than a few seconds. However, there is one Dugong near Bundaberg that has been seen so many times by divers and snorkellers over the last decade that it has been nicknamed Dougie.

Dougie smiles for the author's camera.

I first encountered Dougie in 2014 on a dive off Barolin Rocks, at Coral Cove. I had heard tales of a Dugong that drops in on divers, but after a dozen dives at the site I had never seen the animal. Then, on a memorable day in October that year, Dougie paid me a quick visit. I was photographing a sea snake when Dougie silently swam up beside me. The Dugong slowly swam around me, closely inspecting me for several seconds, until a turtle suddenly took off and startled Dougie and it swam off.

I didn't see Dougie again until 2019, when I had two wonderful visits over two days at Barolin Rocks. On the first day it was a quick visit, with the Dugong giving me the once over and departing. But on the second day the encounter lasted for more than five minutes, with us swimming along side-by-side and even lying on the sandy bottom together. It was an unforgettable encounter, being only at arm's length from a normally shy mammal.

Encounters with Dougie are very unpredictable, and it is possible that more than one Dugong visits the site. I have a feeling that the one I encountered was the same Dugong, and judging by its size I suspect Dougie is a female rather than a male, and should perhaps be renamed Dougette.

THE SPECIES

Baleen Whales

Whales are split into two groups based on their dental arrangement and feeding method. There are the toothed whales, which have teeth, and the baleen whales that lack teeth and instead have bristles in their mouth called baleen.

Baleen whales are filter feeders, consuming a variety of tiny prey like krill, copepods and small fish. The baleen is arranged in plates in the upper jaw and forms a thick bristle-like net to capture food particles. These whales ingest large quantities of water and then expel the water through the baleen to trap prey.

Baleen whales are generally very large, some of the largest animals to have ever lived. There are 16 species of baleen whales, with four family groups based on similar characteristics. Three of these families are found in Australian waters – the right whales, the rorqual whales and the Pygmy Right Whale, which is placed in its own family.

SOUTHERN RIGHT WHALE *Eubalaena australis*

Only found in the Southern Hemisphere, this is one of the world's three right whale species. They were called 'right whales' by whalers because they were the right whales to kill, as they were slow swimmers, found close to shore and had plenty of meat and oil.

Right whales are easily distinguished from other baleen whales by the white crusty callosities on the head. The Southern Right Whale also lacks a dorsal fin. They are a grey to black colour, can grow to 18m long and weight up to 90 tonnes, with the males slightly smaller than the females. This species generally lives to be around 70 years old, however recent research discovered that some live to be 150 years old.

Long-distance migrants

These whales spend the summer in Antarctica, feeding on zooplankton and krill. Over winter they migrate north, with populations seen off southern Africa, South America, New Zealand and Australia. While in Australian waters they breed and give birth, after a 12-month gestation period. The females give birth in shallow bays, with the newborn calf around 4m to 6m long. Calves stay with their mother for around a year, drinking lots of milk over the winter months so they can fatten up for the trip back to Antarctica.

In Australia, Southern Right Whales are observed between June and November, from southern Western Australia to southern New South Wales. South Australia is the best place to observe the species, especially in the Great Australian Bight and off Victor Harbour. These slow-moving whales often enter shallow bays and harbours, and some are curious of boats and people. They regularly breach and tail sail, raising their flukes out of the water.

It is estimated that the Southern Right Whale population is about half of what it was before whaling and it is listed as Least Concern by CITES (the Convention on International Trade in Endangered Species). About 5,000 visit Australian waters each year.

Southern Right Whale female and calf. John Natoli

PYGMY RIGHT WHALE *Caperea marginata*

Growing to 6.5m long and weighing up to 4 tonnes, this is the smallest of the baleen whales and one that is rarely seen. It is actually not a right whale, but are more closely related to rorqual whales such as the minke whales.

Little is known about the Pygmy Right Whale. Like many other baleen whales, it spends the summer in Antarctica feeding on krill and copepods. Over winter the species migrates north and is found around the southern coastline of Australia. It is grey above and has a white belly, a small dorsal fin and a white chevron-shaped patch behind the eye, like the minke whales. This has made identifying this species difficult.

Very few of these rare whales have been seen in Australian waters. A few have washed up on beaches around Tasmania, and groups and individuals have been spotted off the coastline. They have also been observed with other whales and dolphins. The species was rarely hunted by whalers and its population is unknown, although its conservation status is listed as Least Concern.

Antarctic Minke Whale. Shutterstock

ANTARCTIC MINKE WHALE *Balaenoptera bonaerensis*

The minke whales are small rorqual whales with the family containing two recognised species and several subspecies. The Antarctic Minke Whale is found around Antarctica during the summer months, where it feeds on krill and small fishes. Over winter it migrates north to warmer tropical waters and is seen off many Southern Hemisphere countries, including Australia.

It grows to 12m long and weighs up to 12 tonnes. A very slender and streamlined whale, with a pointed snout and small dorsal fin, this species can reach a top speed of 40km/h. Antarctic Minke Whales are grey to black in colour on top with a white belly; they also have pale grey streaks on the body and fins.

Over winter they travel to warm tropical waters to breed and give birth. The calves are 2.7m long at birth, after a 10-month gestation period, and stay with the mother for around six months.

This species of minke whale is rarely seen in Australian waters, except off Western Australia. They were the last whale to be killed in large numbers and continued to be killed after whaling ended in so-called scientific whaling. The population of Antarctic Minke Whales is thought to be around half a million and the species is listed as Near Threatened.

DWARF MINKE WHALE *Balaenoptera acutorostrata*

The most common minke whale seen in Australian waters. Currently it is considered a subspecies of the Common Minke Whale, which is found in the Northern Hemisphere, however, many researchers believe that it should be classified as a new species of minke whale.

Growing to only 8m long, it is much smaller than other minkes. These whales have the most complex colour patterns of any baleen whale. They have a dark grey back and white belly, but also have light grey patches on the head and sides and white patches on the pectoral fins, the shoulder and snout.

Dwarf Minke Whales feed in Antarctica over summer and head to warmer tropical waters over winter. In Australia they are seen off both the west and east coast, but are mostly seen on the Great Barrier Reef between March and October. They come to these warmer waters to breed and give birth, with the calves around 2m long at birth. These whales can give birth once a year, unlike most other baleen whales that only have a calf every two to four years.

WHALE SONG

The Humpback Whale is famous for its haunting songs. However, all the baleen whales make moans, groans and other noises that can be heard underwater. Most of these sounds are low, deep rumbles that sound very alien-like. The Dwarf Minke Whale makes the most unusual noise – an industrial-like 'da-da-daaaang' that is known as the Star Wars sound!

The Dwarf Minke is the most friendly and curious of all the whales. While on the Great Barrier Reef they seek out boats and often stay around them for hours at a time. Dive boats have taken advantage of this and offer special whale snorkels with the Dwarf Minke Whales each June and July on the Ribbon Reefs, north of Cairns.

Dwarf Minke Whale.

BRYDE'S WHALE / EDEN'S WHALE
Balaenoptera brydei / B. edeni

The Bryde's Whale is a medium-sized rorqual whale found in tropical to warm temperate waters around the world. Pronounced 'broo-dess', this whale has several subspecies and in recent years three of these subspecies have been described as new whale species. One of these is the Eden's Whale, which is most likely the Bryde's species seen in Australia.

Growing to a length of 15m, the Eden's Whale has short pectoral fins, a small dorsal fin and a narrow-pointed snout. This species looks very similar to many other rorqual whales, but is distinguished by three parallel ridges on its head, between the snout and blowhole. Like many other rorqual whales it has numerous throat grooves that allow the throat to expand when feeding. Eden's Whales can weigh up to 25 tonnes.

Lunging for fish

Eden's Whales feed on schools of small fish, zooplankton and cephalopods like squid. They are attracted to bait balls of fish, which also attract dolphins, sharks, birds and tuna, and lunge into the feeding frenzy of predators to get their share.

There is no set breeding or birthing time for Eden's Whales. They have a 12-month gestation, with the calves around 4m long at birth, and breed every second year. The calf is nursed by the mother for 6–12 months.

Eden's Whales are occasionally seen around the Australian coastline. They are mostly seen off the east coast and are sometimes observed by whale-watching boats. More than 30,000 Bryde's Whales were killed before whaling ceased, and today their population is thought to be around 100,000. The species is listed as Least Concern.

Feeding Bryde's Whale. Shutterstock/Sapikusan

Sei Whale. Shutterstock/Martin Prochazkacz

SEI WHALE *Balaenoptera borealis*

Preferring oceanic waters, this species rarely ventures close to the coast and consequently is not often seen. The third-largest whale species, it grows to 19.5m long and can weigh up to 28 tonnes. One of the fastest whales, it can reach speeds of 50km/h in short bursts.

A dark grey colour, the Sei Whale also has pale grey markings across its back and sides. Its head has a single ridge from the snout to the blowhole, which is a distinguishing feature. It also has shorter throat ridges than other rorqual whales, as it mostly feeds by skimming at the surface for krill, copepods and zooplankton, and not lunging like other baleen whales.

It is found in subpolar regions in summer and temperate to subtropical waters in winter. They generally avoid polar and tropical waters, and the northern and southern populations are recognised as separate subspecies.

Sei Whales breed and birth during winter, with the calf around 4.5m long at birth. Little is known about the behaviour or social lives of these whales. They are sometimes seen in groups and can live to be 70 years old. In Australian waters they are occasionally seen by whale-watching boats during winter.

Commercial whaling killed more than 200,000 of these whales. The population today is around 50,000, and the species is still listed as Endangered.

FIN WHALE *Balaenoptera physalus*

This species has a hook-like dorsal fin like other rorqual whales, but also a distinct ridge behind this fin. These huge whales grow to 26m long and can weigh up 81 tonnes, making them the second largest of all the whales.

These whales are a dark grey colour with a paler V-shaped chevron behind the head. Fin Whales also have an asymmetrical pattern on the head, with white on the lower right side and black on lower left. This species is found around the planet, with the northern and southern populations recognised as separate subspecies.

Fin Whales consume schools of small fish, squid, krill and copepods. They spend the summer in polar regions and migrate during winter to temperate and tropical regions. These whales breed every two to three years, and the 6m-long calves are born after a 12-month gestation. They can live to be more than 100 years old.

They travel and feed in groups that can vary in size from five to 20. With a larger population in the Northern Hemisphere, they are more commonly seen in this area than they are in the south. Sightings of Fin Whales are rare in Australian waters.

Commercial whaling had a heavy impact on Fin Whale numbers, with more than 700,000 killed in southern waters alone. Today the population is around 100,000 and the species is listed as Vulnerable.

RORQUAL HYBRIDS

Fin Whales and Blue Whales are known to interbreed and produced hybrid offspring that are capable of reproducing. This interbreeding is thought to be a result of whaling drastically depleting their numbers.

Fin Whale. Shutterstock/Juan Gracia

Blue Whale.

BLUE WHALE *Balaenoptera musculus*

The majestic Blue Whale is the largest animal ever to have lived, reaching a length of 30m and weigh up to 200 tonnes. However, being extremely large didn't prevent whalers from slaughtering them, in fact they almost hunted them to extinction. Today the population of Blue Whales is between 10,000 and 25,000 and the species is listed as Endangered.

This immense whale has a greyish-blue mottled colouration across the back and sides and a yellowish-white belly. It has a small dorsal fin and a U-shaped head, unlike the V-shaped head of the Fin Whale. Blue Whales feed almost exclusively on krill.

These whales feed in polar regions during summer and visit tropical waters to breed and birth in winter. However, there are numerous Blue Whale subspecies and some of these have shorter migration routes, with some avoiding polar regions and instead visiting temperate zones during summer.

They take about 10 years to reach sexual maturity and breed every two to three years. They have a ten-to-twelve-month gestation, and the calf is around 6m long at birth. The calf grows very quickly, feasting on its mother's rich milk and growing to around 16m long before being weaned at six to eight months of age.

Little is known about the social lives of Blue Whales. They are mostly seen alone, but can form into groups when feeding, mating or migrating. Off Australia, the Pygmy Blue Whale (*Balaenoptera musculus* ssp. *brevicauda*) is the form most commonly seen by people. This subspecies grows to 24m long and spends the winter in Indonesia, migrating to the southern waters of Australia in summer. The best places to see Blue Whales in Australia is off southern Western Australia and Victoria.

Humpback Whale female and calf.

HUMPBACK WHALE *Megaptera novaeangliae*

The most famous baleen whale. While most other whales are shy and discreet, the Humpback is a complete show-off that loves to breach, tail slap, pectoral wave, spy hop and sunbake on the surface, which has made it the most popular cetacean with whale-watching trips.

Very distinct from its rorqual whale cousins, the Humpback has oversized pectoral fins and bumps on its head and flippers called tubercles. Growing to 17m long and weighing up to 40 tonnes, they have a black back and sides, and a white and black belly, that is more white than black in the southern population.

Humpbacks spend the winter in polar regions feeding on krill, copepods and small fishes. They migrate to tropical and subtropical regions during winter to breed and give birth. Females have an 11-month gestation and give birth every second year. The calves are 4.3m long at birth and stay with their mother for around one year.

Favouring inshore waters and sheltered bays, especially when they have suckling calves, Humpbacks were heavily targeted by whalers. Commercial whaling devastated their numbers, reducing the population to less than 5,000. Today the population is around 135,000 and the species is listed as Least Concern.

This is the easiest whale to see off the coast of Australia. Each winter large populations migrate up and down the east and west coast, and many are so close to shore they can be observed from beaches and headlands. Numerous whale-watching boats operate during the season, allowing for very close encounters with these impressive whales.

BUBBLE NETTING

Humpback Whales feed like other rorqual whales, opening their mouths wide at the surface to gulp down vast quantities of tiny prey. However, they also use a very clever technique to bunch their prey together called bubble netting. Rising from a depth of 20m, the whales expel air from their blowhole as they spiral towards the surface, creating a large circle of bubbles to entrap their prey.

Toothed Whales And Dolphins

These predatory cetaceans have teeth to bite, catch and consume a variety of prey. This group contains several whale families, as well as the dolphins and porpoises.

Most toothed whales have conical teeth that are designed to catch fish or squid, or other marine mammals in the case of Killer Whales. While toothed whales generally have good vision, they don't rely on their eyes to find prey and navigate, as they also have excellent hearing and echolocation.

There are 73 toothed whale species, split into 10 family groups. The best known of these families are the sperm whales and the oceanic dolphins, with this family containing all the common dolphins and Killer Whale. However, other families include the beaked whales, river dolphins, Beluga and Narwhal.

SPERM WHALE *Physeter macrocephalus*

Made famous by the book *Moby Dick*, the Sperm Whale is the largest toothed whale and the largest predator on Earth. These whales have impressive diving skills and can hold their breath for one hour as they search for Giant Squid.

They grow to 16m long and weigh up to 45 tonnes, with the male about 5m longer than the female and up to three times heavier. These distinctive-looking whales have a large blunt head and an underslung jaw. They are grey in colour, and some have blotchy patterns. They also have wrinkly skin, unlike the smooth skin of other whales.

The Sperm Whale has the largest brain of any animal, five times heavier than an average human brain. They are also very social, with females and calves living in pods and working together to protect and feed their young. Young males live in bachelor groups, while older males are generally solitary, only encountering other males to fight for breeding rights. Sperm Whales often rub against each other and communicate with a series of clicks called codas.

Sperm Whale. Shutterstock/Martin Prochazkacz

Sperm Whale has a distinctive bulging head and narrow lower jaw. Shutterstock/Martin Prochazkacz

Diving deep for squid

They eat a variety of large squid and fish, sharks and rays, diving as deep as 2,250m to hunt prey using echolocation. In their head is a waxy oil mixture called spermaceti that is used to focus their echolocation clicks to find prey in the dark waters of the deep ocean. Many Sperm Whales have scars from battles with Giant Squid.

Found around the world in tropical to subpolar regions, Sperm Whales are very cosmopolitan. These whales live to around 70 years of age and the females give birth every four to twenty years. They have a long pregnancy of 14 to 16 months, and the calves are around 4m long at birth. Calves can suckle up to four years.

These whales rarely visit inshore waters and prefer deep water off the continental shelf. While they are found around Australia, they are mostly seen in offshore canyons, such as the Bremer Canyon off Western Australia.

More than one million Sperm Whales were killed during the days of whaling. Today the population is around 300,000 and the species is listed as Vulnerable.

DEEP SLEEPERS

Sperm Whales are one of the few cetaceans known to regularly sleep. When sleeping the pod of whales hangs in the water near the surface, either head up or head down. Most other whales sleep as they slowly swim, closing down half of their brain and keeping the other half alert.

PYGMY SPERM WHALE *Kogia breviceps*

The Sperm Whale's closest relatives are two relatively tiny whale species that are rarely seen. The Pygmy Sperm Whale is the larger of the two, growing to 3.5m long.

These small whales inhabit temperate and tropical waters around the world, but are shy and elusive of boats and people. When seen at sea they rarely make a splash or blow at the surface, and silently disappear below the waves. In Australia, they are mostly seen along the southern coastline.

The Pygmy Sperm Whale looks like a miniature Sperm Whale, but with a smaller rounded head. It has a bluish-grey back and a pinkish-cream belly. The calves are around 1.2m long at birth. They feed mostly on squid and octopus.

Small numbers of these rare whales are still hunted in Asia and the population size is unknown, although the species is listed as Least Concern.

Pygmy Sperm Whale. Sergio Martinez

DWARF SPERM WHALE *Kogia sima*

This small, rare whale is not often seen. Growing to only 2.7m long, it looks like a Sperm Whale but is only the size of a dolphin.

They feed mostly on squid, but also consume fish and crustaceans, diving to 1,500m to catch prey in deep water off the continental shelf.

These whales are found in tropical and temperate waters around the world and have been seen off Australia a few times. Little is known about their social lives, with the calves measuring around 1m in length at birth.

The Dwarf Sperm Whale population is unknown, and the species is listed as Least Concern. However, they are still hunted in parts of Asia as food and bait.

Dwarf Sperm Whale breaching. Wikimedia Commons/Robert Pitman (NOAA)

GRAY'S BEAKED WHALE *Mesoplodon grayi*

Gray's Beaked Whale. Cassandra Smith

> **A LITTLE-KNOWN FAMILY**
>
> The beaked whales are a rare and little-known family containing 24 species. They vary in size from 4–13m and all have a dolphin-like beak. The only time that beaked whales are generally seen is when they strand. As most beaked whale species are rarely seen or photographed, this book only contains images of half the species seen in Australian waters.

Only found in temperate waters in the Southern Hemisphere, this little-known species occasionally strands on beaches in Australia. It grows to 6m long, has an elongated beak and is generally found in small pods in deep water. The only place in Australia where this species is occasionally seen is the Bremer Canyon off Western Australia, where it is preyed on by Killer Whales. The population size is unknown and its status is listed as Least Concern.

ANDREWS' BEAKED WHALE *Mesoplodon bowdoini*

Another rare species that researchers know little about, this whale grows to 4.9m long and has a short beak. The females are grey with lighter markings on their sides and belly, while the males are a dark grey with a lighter saddle-like pattern on the side. Males typically have lots of scars across the body from fighting other males.

Found in the offshore temperate waters of Australia and New Zealand, little is known about the species' social life or population. It is listed as Least Concern.

RAMARI'S BEAKED WHALE *Mesoplodon eueu*

A recently described species about which little is known. It is found in temperate waters in the Southern Hemisphere and grows to 5m long. This whale has a short beak and is grey with lighter markings on the side. Most of what researchers know about this species has come from stranded individuals.

GINKGO-TOOTHED BEAKED WHALE *Mesoplodon ginkgodens*

Found in tropical and temperate waters of the Pacific and Indian Oceans, these rare and little-known whales occasionally wash up on beaches. They grow to 4.9m long and have a small beak. The female has a light grey back and lighter belly, while the male is dark grey with white spots on the underside of the tail and white patches on the head and beak. These whales feed on squid and their population size is unknown.

Ginkgo-toothed Beaked Whale. Stanley Chan

HECTOR'S BEAKED WHALE *Mesoplodon hectori*

A very rare small whale found only in temperate waters of the Southern Hemisphere. Grows to 4.2m in length and has a short, pointed beak. These poorly studied whales have rarely been seen in the wild, and in Australian waters a few have stranded on beaches in Western Australia and South Australia.

ARNOUX'S BEAKED WHALE *Berardius arnuxii*

Grows to 9.8m in length and only found in the temperate and polar regions of the Southern Hemisphere. This species has a long beak, small flippers and is grey in colour, but generally with lots of white scars across the body. They have been observed in pods in Antarctica, but little is known about the species.

Arnoux's Beaked Whale. Justin Hofman

Dense-beaked Whale. Wikimedia Commons/NOAA Photo Library

DENSE-BEAKED WHALE *Mesoplodon densirostris*

One of the strangest-looking cetaceans, these whales grow to 4.6m long and have a long beak with a curved jawline. In mature males this curved jaw is quite pronounced and features a lower jaw tooth on each side that projects above the beak like a tusk.

Grey to brown above with a white belly, these whales are found around the world in tropical and warm-temperate seas. They feed on small fish and cephalopods, which they suck into their mouth rather than bite.

This species is quite social and always found in small pods. It inhabits offshore waters and is rarely seen in Australia. Little is known about its population and it is listed as Least Concern.

STRAP-TOOTHED BEAKED WHALE *Mesoplodon layardii*

The male is very distinctive, with two tusks that protrude from the lower jaw. These flat tusks can grow to 34cm long and curve over the top of the beak, restricting how far the animal can open its mouth.

Grows to 6.2m long and is found in the Southern Hemisphere in temperate waters. Dark grey with a white cape-like pattern in front of the flippers and across the upper back. Little is known about the species, but these whales are generally seen in small pods and may migrate. They are listed as Least Concern.

SHEPHERD'S BEAKED WHALE *Tasmacetus shepherdi*

Also called the Tasman Whale, as most sighting of this species have been in the Tasman Sea between New Zealand and Australia. These whales grow to 6m long and have a long beak and tusks at the tip of the lower jaw. They are dark grey with a white belly and paler bands around the head, flippers and back. The Shepherd's Beaked Whale lives in deep offshore waters and feeds on fish and squid.

CUVIER'S BEAKED WHALE *Ziphius cavirostris*

The most wide-ranging and the best-known member of the beaked-whale family. Found in tropical and temperate waters around the planet and grows to 6.9m in length.

These whales have a short beak and a robust body. Males are dark grey with

Cuvier's Beaked Whale. Shutterstock/Andrea Izzotti

lighter colouring on the head and sides, while females are grey to brown with limited lighter colouring. The young are around 2m long at birth.

Cuvier's Beaked Whales feed on squid and fish and dive very deep to find food. They can dive to almost 3,000m and the longest recorded dive was for 222 minutes – a record for any mammal.

Occasionally seen off the Australian coastline in deep water. Whale-watching trips to see Killer Whales at Bremer Canyon sometimes find this species, as they feed in these deep waters and fall prey to Killer Whales. The Killer Whales in this area have developed a special hunting technique to locate and kill beaked whales as they surface from a deep feeding dive. Although Cuvier's Beaked Whales were once hunted, today the species is listed as Least Concern.

SOUTHERN BOTTLENOSE WHALE *Hyperoodon planifrons*

Another species of beaked whale. Grows to 7.5m in length and has a short beak and a large melon-shaped forehead. Grey in colour, with males having a white beak.

Found in polar regions of the Southern Hemisphere and appears to migrate into temperate regions such as the coastline of southern Australia. Feeds on squid. Little is known about their behaviour or population.

Southern Bottlenose Whale. Wikimedia Commons/Simon Tonge

KILLER WHALE *Orcinus orca*

Also known as the Orca, this is the largest member of the oceanic dolphin family and one of the fiercest predators in the ocean. Hunting in packs, they can tackle a wide variety of prey, including everything from Great White Sharks to Blue Whales.

With their distinctive black-and-white pattern and rounded head, the Killer Whale is an easy species to identify. These whales grow to 8m long and weight up to 6 tonnes, with the males being longer and larger than the females and having a taller dorsal fin.

Found in all oceans from tropical to polar. There are several subspecies recognised and two main types of Killer Whales – the residents that stay in one area and mostly eat fish, and the transients that migrate from area to area and eat everything from sharks to marine mammals. However, some resident populations also feed on other cetaceans.

Killer Whales are very social and have very complex relationships, with most offspring staying with their mother for life. These matriarch groups temporarily come together to feed and mate,

BRAINY ORCAS

Killer Whales have the second-largest brain of any marine mammal and are quite intelligent. Captive animals are easily trained, and wild Orca teach complex hunting techniques to their young. They are also quick to solve problems, they like to play and are very curious of the world around them.

Killer Whale.

forming into larger pods. Pods can also mix, forming into larger clans.

Females give birth every five years and have a long gestation of 15–18 months. The calves are around 2.5m long at birth. These whales are long lived, with females living to 90 and males to around 60.

Three populations

Three populations of Killer Whales are seen around Australia. The east-coast and west-coast populations roam up and down the coasts, but are not commonly seen as they are mostly offshore and transient. The largest population is found in the deep waters of the Bremer Canyon in Western Australia. With about 300 animals, this is the largest group of Killer Whales in the Southern Hemisphere. They are thought to reside in the waters year-round, feeding on tuna, squid and other whales, and are mostly seen during summer and autumn when special whale-watching trips are run from Bremer Bay.

Even though some Killer Whales kill and eat seals, dolphins and even large whales, they are generally not considered dangerous to humans. In the wild they are very curious of people and sometimes closely interact with swimmers, surfers and snorkellers. However, Killer Whales kept in captivity have killed and injured their keepers.

Killer Whales were taken in some whaling activities, but in some instances they assisted the whalers. The most famous case happened in Eden, New South Wales, where the local Killer Whales would herd baleen whales into Twofold Bay to make it easier for the whalers to catch them. The Killer Whales were rewarded with the tongue and lips of the dead whales.

The global population of Killer Whales is unknown but thought to be at least 50,000 animals.

Pygmy Killer Whale.

PYGMY KILLER WHALE *Feresa attenuata*

This little-known species looks nothing like an Orca. These small cetaceans grow to 2.2m long and are dark grey with a rounded head. They inhabit offshore waters in tropical and subtropical waters around the world.

Pygmy Killer Whales are secretive and shy. They travel in small groups, sometimes with other cetaceans, and rarely make a splash at the surface. They feed on fish and squid, and their population size is unknown. Although they are found in Australia's offshore waters, these whales are rarely seen.

MELON-HEADED WHALE *Peponocephala electra*

Looks similar to the Pygmy Killer Whale, but with a more pointed head. These small cetaceans grow to 2.7m long and are found in tropical and subtropical waters around the world.

These social animals travel in large groups that can number more than 1,000; they often mix with groups of dolphins. They dive to 470m in offshore waters, feeding on fish, squid and crustaceans.

Although not often seen in Australian waters, Melon-headed Whales have mass stranded on beaches. Their population size is unknown, and the species is listed as Least Concern.

Melon-headed Whale. Shutterstock/Ethan Daniels

FALSE KILLER WHALE *Pseudorca crassidens*

Named because it has a skull like an Orca, the False Killer Whale has a much slimmer body and is grey to black in colour. While they have been known to feed on other dolphins and whales, their diet consists mostly of fish and squid.

This is an offshore species found in tropical and temperate seas around the world. They grow to 6m long, with the calves around 2m long at birth, and can live for up to 60 years. These whales are very social and always found in pods of 10–50 animals. They often mix with other dolphin species and have been known to interbreed.

With strong social bonds, False Killer Whales sometimes strand on beaches in large groups. They are occasionally seen off the coastline of Australia. Their population size is unknown and the species is listed as Near Threatened.

False Killer Whale.

Short-finned Pilot Whale.

SHORT-FINNED PILOT WHALE *Globicephala macrorhynchus*

There are two species of pilot whales that received their unusual name from sailors who assumed pods of these cetaceans were piloted by a leader. Both look very similar, with this species having shorter fins, a shorter beak and less teeth.

The Short-finned Pilot Whale is black to dark grey with a robust body, a hooked dorsal fin and a rounded head. They grow to 6m in length, with the male about a metre longer than the female. The calves are around 1.2m long at birth. These whales live for around 45–60 years.

These whales reside in tropical and subtropical waters worldwide. They dive to depths of 1,000m looking for prey and mostly feed on squid, octopus and fish.

They are very social whales and live in large pods that number from 10–30. These family pods are led by an older female, with the females out numbering the males by eight to one. Males temporarily leave the pods to mate with females in other pods.

Although an offshore species, Short-finned Pilot Whales are sometimes seen along the east coast of Australia, even close to shore. They have been known to mass strand on beaches. The population is around 700,000 and the species is listed as Least Concern.

LONG-FINNED PILOT WHALE *Globicephala melas*

Looks almost identical to its cousin the Short-finned Pilot Whale; however, prefers temperate and subpolar waters of the Southern Hemisphere and north Atlantic. This species is slightly larger, with males growing to 7.6m in length and females to 6m.

Very social and always seen in large pods that can vary in number from a dozen to several hundred. Animals in the pod work together when feeding and help to look after calves. These pods often combine with several dolphin species and are known to mass strand on beaches. Feeds on squid and fish that are captured on deep dives.

In Australia these whales are best seen off Victoria, Tasmania and southern Western Australia. They are mostly seen during summer, when they possibly move into warmer waters for the birth of calves. The population size is unknown, but is likely more than one million, and the species is listed as Least Concern.

Long-finned Pilot Whale. Cassandra Smith

RISSO'S DOLPHIN *Grampus griseus*

The natural colouration is dark grey; however most are covered in white markings, which are scars from fighting and interacting with each other. It is thought that the males especially display their scars with pride, as the more scars they have, the more they can impress females and father young.

These large oceanic dolphins have a rounded head, no beak and grow to 4m long. Found worldwide in tropical and subtropical waters, and sometimes venture into temperate waters. They are always seen in groups, and feed on cephalopods and some fishes. Risso's Dolphins only have two to seven pairs of teeth in their lower jaw, and these are thought to be mainly used in mating conflicts, and to inflict scars.

This shy species is not often seen. It prefers offshore waters and in Australia is mostly seen off New South Wales and southern Queensland. The population size is unknown, and the species is listed as Least Concern.

Risso's Dolphin showing battle scars. Shutterstock/Tory Kallman

AUSTRALIAN SNUBFIN DOLPHIN *Orcaella heinsohni*

Described as a new species in 2005, as previously it had been confused with the Irrawaddy Dolphin (*Orcaella brevirostris*) of Asia. This small, rare dolphin is found in the tropical coastal waters of northern Australia.

Growing to 2.7m long, it has a rounded head, no beak, a small dorsal fin and a neck crease. They are brownish-grey in colour and at the surface can be mistaken for a Dugong.

Australian Snubfin Dolphins are usually seen in small groups and feed in murky shallow waters, often around mangroves. They prey on fishes and cephalopods, are thought to live for around 30 years.

Sometimes seen off Broome and the Kimberley coast in Western Australia. The population size is unknown, and the species is listed as Vulnerable.

Australian Snubfin Dolphin. Lisa Mazzella

AUSTRALIAN HUMPBACK DOLPHIN *Sousa sahulensis*

This is one of several humpback dolphins that were once thought to be a single species. It is found in the tropical and subtropical waters of northern Australia, where it inhabits shallow bays, estuaries and mangroves.

Growing to 2.7m long, it has a small dorsal fin, a long beak and is grey in colour with a lighter grey to pink beak and belly. Feeds mostly on fish. These dolphins have been known to drive prey into very swallow water and beach themselves, before wriggling back into the water.

These social animals are found in small pods. Females breed every three years and calves are born after a 10- to 12-month gestation period. They are thought to live for around 30 years.

This shy species avoids people and boats. In Australia the best place to see them is Tin Can Bay, Queensland, where a pod has been hand fed for many years.

With a population of 10,000, which is in decline due to habit loss, pollution and fishing pressures, the Australian Humpback Dolphin is listed as Vulnerable.

Australian Humpback Dolphin.

Rough-toothed Dolphin. Shutterstock/Buchpetzer

ROUGH-TOOTHED DOLPHIN *Steno bredanensis*

Named for the ridges on its teeth, this offshore dolphin is found in tropical and subtropical waters around the world but is rarely seen.

Reaching a length of 2.8m, it has a conical head and slender beak, with a dark grey back, a lighter grey flank and a white lower jaw. Usually lives in groups of 10–20 but can be also be seen in larger groups or alone. These dolphins mostly feed on fish and dive to around 50m when hunting prey.

Sightings of this species in Australian waters are rare, and little is known about the population.

DUSKY DOLPHIN *Lagenorhynchus obscurus*

This small cetacean grows to 1.8m in length and has a short beak and a dark grey to black back with white panels on the face and sides. Found in temperate and subpolar regions of the Southern Hemisphere and prefers inshore waters.

Dusky Dolphins are social and always found in groups. Several groups can come together when feeding on fish and squid. They are one of the most acrobatic dolphins, and often leap from the water and perform twists, spins, backslaps and somersaults. The youngsters learn this behaviour from their mothers.

Dusky Dolphin. Shutterstock/Don Mammoser

Only rarely seen off Australia. It is thought that those seen off southern Australia may be visitors from New Zealand as the species is far more common in New Zealand waters. The population size is unknown, and the species is listed as Least Concern.

FRASER'S DOLPHIN *Lagenodelphis hosei*

Found in tropical waters around the globe, these dolphins form into large groups that number from 100 to more than 1,000, although they shy away from boats and flee in an explosion of splashes.

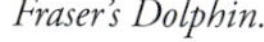

Fraser's Dolphin.

This species grows to 2.7m long and has a short beak and dorsal fin. They have a grey back and a white or pink belly, and some have a darker stripe between these two colours. Feed on fish, shrimps and squid and have been known to dive to depths of 500m.

Fraser's Dolphins are rare in Australia's tropical north. They are an offshore species with an unknown population and are listed as Least Concern.

COMMON BOTTLENOSE DOLPHIN *Tursiops truncatus*

The best-known dolphin species in the world, being the star of films, television shows and captive displays in oceanariums. While found around the world in tropical and temperate waters, this is an offshore species in Australian waters, so rarely seen.

Growing to 4m long, this is quite a large dolphin. It is grey with a short beak and a hooked dorsal fin. This species also has a flexible neck, unlike other dolphins that have five of their vertebrae fused together, giving them a ridge neck. They are found in inshore and offshore waters and several subspecies are recognised.

Common Bottlenose Dolphins are very social and usually found in groups varying in size from 15 to several hundred animals. However, groups can vary – sometimes just a pair is seen, or groups of adult males, nursing mothers or subadults. Calves are around 1.4m long at birth and suckle for up to 20 months. Calves stay with their mother for up to eight years, with the females breeding every three to five years.

Like all dolphins they use echolocation to find prey. They feed on fish, squid and shrimps, hunting individually or as a group that works together to herd

Common Bottlenose Dolphin. Shutterstock/Carolyn Hill

Indo-Pacific Bottlenose Dolphin.

schools of fish. They don't use their teeth to chew, and instead swallow food whole. However, they use their teeth to grab other dolphins on the fins and tail, which is thought to be a form of communication, but leaves distinctive scars that are used by researchers to identify individuals.

The population is thought to be around 600,000 and the species is listed as Least Concern.

INDO-PACIFIC BOTTLENOSE DOLPHIN *Tursiops aduncus*

The most common dolphin seen in Australia. Found throughout the Indo-West Pacific in both tropical and temperate waters.

Growing to 2.6m long, the Indo-Pacific Bottlenose Dolphin is smaller than the Common Bottlenose Dolphin. It may look similar, but it is more slender, and has a longer beak and irregular spots on its belly and sides. This species also has more teeth, and enjoys a diet of fish, crustaceans and cephalopods. These dolphins also scavenge, following fishing vessels to gather by-catch and even taking food from people.

These very social dolphins live in groups that vary in size from five to several hundred. They also mix with other dolphin species. This species breeds and births in spring and summer, with the 1.3m-long calf born after a 12-month gestation period. Calves are weaned

FINDING FOOD

Indo-Pacific Bottlenose Dolphins are quite clever and use their intelligence and echolocation to find prey, even when it is hidden under a layer of sand. In Shark Bay, Western Australia, the local dolphins pluck sponges growing on the seafloor to cover their beak when probing the sand for food.

by two years of age but stay with their mother for up to five years.

People can view these dolphins at many places around Australia. They are common inshore, found in bays, beaches, estuaries and even harbours. There are several places where wild groups are hand feed, most notably at Monkey Mia in Western Australia and Tangalooma off Brisbane.

This species is kept in captivity, and impacted by fishing practices, pollution and habitat loss. The population size is unknown, and the species is listed as Near Threatened.

PANTROPICAL SPOTTED DOLPHIN *Stenella attenuata*

The world's second-most-common cetacean species, with a population of more than three million. However, a few decades ago the population crashed after millions were killed in fishing nets designed to catch tuna. Fortunately, after an outcry from environmental groups and the public, safer nets were introduced and dolphin-safe tuna hit supermarkets.

These slender dolphins grow to 2.6m in length and have a small dorsal fin and a long thin beak. They are grey in colour with lighter greys on the head and flank. As they age, they develop lighter-coloured spots. They feed on small fish and cephalopods and are always seen in groups.

Found in tropical and subtropical waters around the globe, Pantropical Spotted Dolphins are found in inshore and offshore waters, with the offshore dolphins generally larger. These dolphins follow schools of tuna, as they feed on the same small fishes. In Australian waters they are occasional seen off Queensland and New South Wales but are considered uncommon.

With its large population the status of this species is listed as Least Concern.

Pantropical Spotted Dolphin. Shutterstock/Pascale Gueret

Spinner Dolphin.

SPINNER DOLPHIN *Stenella longirostris*

The name is apt as they love to spin when they leap from the water. They can perform up to seven spins before they re-enter the water, and this spinning is thought to dislodge remora fish that stick to them, and also to help them communicate with other dolphins.

This small species grow to 2.3m in length and is found in large groups in tropical seas around the world. It is an offshore species that feeds on fish and squid, mostly at night, although some visit inshore waters by day to rest. It has a long beak, a dark grey back and a lighter grey flank and belly.

Spinner Dolphins live in family groups that mix with other families and other dolphins. Several subspecies are recognised. Calves are around 0.7m long when born after a 10-month gestation period, and nursed for one to two years.

In Australian waters these dolphins are mostly seen on the Great Barrier Reef, Queensland, and Ningaloo Reef, Western Australia. The population size is unknown and the species is listed as Least Concern.

STRIPED DOLPHIN *Stenella coeruleoalba*

An offshore species of tropical and temperate waters worldwide. They look like several other small dolphins, having a dark grey back and pale grey sides. However, this species is easily distinguished by a thin dark stripe that runs from the beak and through the eye and then splits to continue down the flank and to the flippers.

Striped Dolphins grow to 2.6m in length and are thought to live to 60 years of age. The females have calves every three to four years, with the young 1m long at birth. These very social dolphins are always seen in large groups and enjoy leaping from the water when on the move and performing tailspins and somersaults.

Diving to depths of 700m, they consume fish, crustaceans and cephalopods. This species is known to mass strand on beaches and is prone to suffering from cetacean morbillivirus, a virus that can weaken the immune system.

In Australia, Striped Dolphins are best seen off southern Western Australia, especially in the waters off Perth and in the Bremer Canyon. Worldwide their population is thought to be around two million and the species is listed as Least Concern.

Striped Dolphin.

Common Dolphins.

COMMON DOLPHIN *Delphinus delphis*

The most abundant cetacean in the world with a population of around six million. It is common in temperate and tropical seas around the planet.

Grows to 2.5m in length and has a dark grey back with a cream to light grey lower flank. Several subspecies are recognised, with the beak size varying between populations. Always seen in groups, which vary in size from dozens to several thousand; these groups consist of females with calves, bachelor males and mix groups of adults. Unlike most other dolphin species, these groups don't consist of closely related family members.

Common Dolphins inhabit both inshore and offshore waters and feed on small fish and cephalopods. They often interact with other dolphin species and have been known to interbreed. The calves are around 1m long at birth, with females mating every one to three years.

Although seen in tropical waters elsewhere, in Australia Common Dolphins are mostly seen in cooler temperate waters. They are often seen in southern Australia's offshore waters and enjoy bow riding boats. This species is listed as Least Concern.

SOUTHERN RIGHT WHALE DOLPHIN *Lissodelphis peronii*

A strange-looking cetacean that lacks a dorsal fin. Growing to 2.5m long, they have a short beak and are mostly white in colour with a thick black curved stripe along the back. Only found in the Southern Hemisphere, ranging from temperate seas to Subantarctic waters.

These dolphins live in offshore waters and are always seen in groups. They dive to depths of 200m to feed on fish and squid. This species is very rare off southern Australia, and only a small number have been sighted. Little is known about this species, although it is listed as Least Concern.

Southern Right Whale Dolphin. Toby Dickson

Seals

The cooler temperate waters of southern Australia are home to many seals. They are mostly seen on offshore islands, but also visit bays to feed and beaches and headlands to rest and sunbake. Some seals also mix with people, visiting popular beaches and jetties, and one even took up residence on the foreshore beside Sydney Opera House.

Three species of seals live, feed, roost and breed in Australian waters, while a further three species also visit Australian shores from time to time.

AUSTRALIAN FUR SEAL *Arctocephalus pusillus doriferus*

This is a subspecies of the Brown Fur Seal (*Arctocephalus pusillus*), which is found off southern Africa. In Australian waters these seals are most common off Victoria and Tasmania, where large breeding colonies are found, with smaller non-breeding colonies occurring off southern New South Wales and South Australia.

The largest member of the fur seal family, the male grows to 2.2m in length, while the female is much smaller and slimmer and grows to 1.8m. The male is brown to dark grey with a darker mane and lighter belly, while the female is light brown to grey with a darker belly and back and a lighter throat.

Australian Fur Seals have large canine-like teeth and feed on fish, octopus, squid and crustaceans. They can dive to 200m to catch prey and hold their breath for up to seven minutes. While graceful, fast and highly manoeuvrable in the water, they are a little clumsy on land, walking, waddling and hopping with the aid of their flippers.

Fur-seal gatherings

These seals spend much of their time in the water, often in groups when looking for prey. They come back to shore to rest, and each October they visit breeding colonies to mate. The males arrive first and establish their territory, fighting other males to claim their patch of turf.

Pregnant females arrive between October and December, then give birth to one or two pups from the last breeding season. They then mate with the dominant male in their area and raise their pups during the summer and autumn. The pups are left unattended for days at a time while the mother goes to sea to feed, and are weaned by six months.

Seal colonies are very noisy

OUTSMARTING SHARKS

Great White Sharks feed on fur seals, but the seals don't make it easy for the sharks. A seal can easily outswim and outmanoeuvre a shark if it is spotted, and even chase and nip the shark. To avoid unseen sharks the seals swim in groups, constantly jumping in and out of the water and randomly darting in different directions.

Australian Fur Seal.

and smelly places, and best viewed from the safety of a boat. Numerous Australian Fur Seal colonies can be seen in southern Australia, with some of the most famous ones being Montague Island in New South Wales and Lady Julia Percy Island in Victoria. People can even snorkel with the seals at some locations.

The population of Australian Fur Seal is around 120,000 and the species is listed as Least Concern.

LONGNOSE FUR SEAL *Arctocephalus forsteri*

The species has a number of common names; however, Longnose Fur Seal is the most widely accepted name for this species in Australia. These seals are found in both Australia and New Zealand, with the largest Australian populations found off southern Western Australia and South Australia. However, they are also seen off Victoria, Tasmania and New South Wales.

Only slightly smaller than the Australian Fur Seal, with males growing to 2m in length. Telling the two species apart is not easy. They differ from their cousins in have a more pointed snout and lighter-coloured whiskers. The Longnose Fur Seal has a grey to brown coat with a lighter belly. Like all fur seals they also have external ears and hind flippers that can rotate forward to help them to walk.

This is the most accomplished diver among the fur seal species, able to dive to depths of 380m and hold their breath for up to 15 minutes. Their diet includes fish, cephalopods and even seabirds. Pups start to learn to dive and forage at about six months of age but are not weaned until about 11 months old.

Similar to Australian Fur Seals, they breed over summer, with the males establishing territories and the females pupping and mating between November and January. The pups often congregate into groups and play together in rock pools when their mothers are off feeding.

Best observed off Albany, Western Australia, and Eaglehawk Neck, Tasmania. The population numbers around 58,000 in Australian waters and the species is listed as Least Concern.

Longnose Fur Seal.

AUSTRALIAN SEA LION *Neophoca cinerea*

While all fur seals and sea lions are curious of people, especially when you snorkel with them, this species deserves the title of 'world's friendliest seal'. These animals are a joy to snorkel with and take great pleasure in zooming around or just lying on the bottom and staring at you. However, they also have the sad distinction of being one of the most endangered seal species.

The male grows to 2.2m in length and is dark brown with a yellow mane. The female grows to 1.8m and has a light grey back and a cream-coloured belly. Today this species is only found off Western Australia and South Australia, but once it was more widespread. Sixty-six small breeding colonies are known, and most are located on offshore islands.

These seals eat a variety of fishes, cephalopods, crustaceans and even Little Penguins. They mostly forage for food on inshore reefs and bays but will travel up to 300km away from their normal colony site.

This species has a strange non-annual breeding cycle that is unique among seals. Breeding can take place anytime between January and June, and the females have a very long gestation period of 14 months and nurse their pups for up to 17 months. Males don't establish a territory, but still fight among themselves to establish a hierarchy.

These sea lions can be seen in many places, including Kangaroo Island. Guided tours to snorkel with them are allowed at sites such as Hopkins Island off Port Lincoln, South Australia, and Jurien Bay, Western Australia.

Australian Sea Lions face many threats, with commercial fishing practices killing far too many each year. They survived sealers, but in the last four decades their numbers have sadly declined by 60 per cent. Today the population is less than 14,000 and the species is listed as Endangered.

Australian Sea Lion.

Subantarctic Fur Seal. Shutterstock/MickaelLG33

SUBANTARCTIC FUR SEAL *Arctocephalus tropicalis*

As its name suggests, this seal inhabits the Subantarctic islands of the Southern Ocean. While they breed, feed and rest on and around these islands, they also travel vast distances in search of food and often end up in temperate zones, including the waters off southern Australia.

The male grows to 2m in length and has a dark grey to brown back, a light brown belly and a distinctive black cap on the head. Females are a light grey to brown and grow to 1.4m.

They feed at night on squid, fish and crustaceans, but are also known to prey on seabirds. These seals travel incredible distances when feeding, and some have been found more than 6,000km from the nearest colony. In southern Australia they can turn up on beaches, islands and headlands, where they generally rest for a few days before moving on.

The population is thought to be around 300,000 and the species is listed as Least Concern.

Southern Elephant Seal. Sandra Broom

SOUTHERN ELEPHANT SEAL *Mirounga leonina*

This is the largest seal species and a true seal. The male is huge, growing to 5.8m in length and weighing almost 4 tonnes. They are up to six times the weight of the female, which grows to 3m in length. This enormous difference between the males and females is the greatest example of sexual dimorphism seen in any mammal.

These seals are very distinctive – not only are they large in size, but they also have large round eyes and the male has an oversized nose that looks like a small elephant's trunk. They use this nose to produce loud roars during the breeding season. Southern Elephant Seals have small flippers and move slowly on land by pushing their body forward. They are very accomplished divers that can hold their breath for almost two hours and dive to depths of 2,388m. They use their whiskers to detect prey and feed on fish, cephalopods and crustaceans.

Southern Elephant Seals inhabit the Subantarctic islands of the Southern Ocean in colonies that can number in the thousands. However, they mostly feed around Antarctica. Each September the breeding season starts with the arrival of the males, who fight for territory. These battles are quite spectacular and bloody, with the combatants lifting themselves vertically and battering against each other, using their teeth to inflict wounds. The males defend their patch, and harem of females, for three months and don't feed during this period.

The females arrive and give birth to last season's pups. The pups are weaned after 23 days, then the females mate and depart to feed. The abandoned pups stay in groups, remaining until they lose their birth coat and can swim and feed for themselves.

These seals come ashore to moult after the breeding season. When moulting some leave the colony and venture north, ending up on beaches in southern

Australia. They often stay for days or weeks, and while some are happy to remain on the beach and sunbake, others like to explore and make a nuisance of themselves on roads and in towns, becoming local celebrities.

The population is thought to be around 740,000 and the species is listed as Least Concern.

LEOPARD SEAL *Hydrurga leptonyx*

One of the top predators of the Southern Ocean, these elongated true seals have a large mouth and very large sharp teeth, like those of a big cat. They feed on fish, cephalopods, seabirds, penguins and even other seals.

They grow to 3.5m in length, with the females slightly longer than the males. They have a slim elongated body and a large head. The dark grey back and light grey belly have a scattered pattern of spots. These seals spend most of their lives around Antarctica, hunting in the pack ice. However, they also visit Subantarctic islands and the southern coastline of Australia during the winter months. Leopard Seals are potentially dangerous and have attacked and bitten people on land and in the water.

They breed and give birth on the pack ice during the summer months. The female digs a hole in the ice for the pup, which is weaned after one month. These are solitary animals that don't form into breeding colonies and little is known about their reproductive behaviour.

The population size is largely unknown, although estimates place the number between 220,000 to 440,000, and the species is listed as Least Concern.

Leopard Seal. Sandra Broom

Sea Cows

The Dugong is the only member of the sea cow family found in the waters of tropical Australia. This is the most common and wide-ranging member of this small family, and it is found throughout the Indo-West Pacific, with northern Australia home to the largest population of these unusual marine mammals.

DUGONG *Dugong dugon*

Grazing on seagrasses in shallow bays, the Dugong is one of the most unusual and unique marine mammals. Growing to 4m long, but rarely reaching more than 3m in length, it has a tail like a dolphin, an elongated and robust body with no dorsal fin, small pectoral fins and a downturned snout with a mouth that appears to have a permanent smile.

Dugongs have small eyes and poor eyesight, so they use their sense of smell and the whiskers on their snout to find

DUGONG TALK

Dugongs communicate with each other using a variety of sounds, including barks, chirps and whistles. Mothers and calves also communicate by regularly touching each other.

Dugong.

food. They have simple peg-like teeth that are perfect for chewing on seagrasses. However, they use their muscular upper lip to pull out the seagrass before they chew it. Dugongs have also been known to eat algae, sea jellies, sea squirts and a range of small invertebrates. Their consumption of seagrasses is like mowing and promotes growth and keeps the seagrasses healthy. Unfortunately, pollution and habitat destruction has seen a reduction of seagrasses in many areas.

Living to 70 years of age, Dugong don't reach sexual maturity until they are eight years old, but some don't breed until they reach 18. They are social animals, but spend a lot of time solitary, only coming together to feed and breed. In the breeding season males establish territories and fight off other males, impressing females with their strength and vigour. After a 13-to-15-month gestation, the female gives birth to a 1.2m long calf. The young stay close to their mother and nurse for up to 18 months. The females have calves every three to seven years, but only have a small number of calves during their lifetime.

Warm-water specialists

Dugongs live in warm shallow bays where seagrasses grow. They are known to migrate to find food and to find warmer water over winter. In Australia Dugongs can be seen in many bays, with Moreton Bay, off Brisbane, and Shark Bay in Western Australia two of the best places to see them.

While Australia still has a healthy Dugong population, their numbers have declined in most other countries which has them listed as Vulnerable. It is estimated that the Dugong population in around 85,000.

INDEX